Spelling
Activity Book

for ages 5-6

This CGP book is bursting with fun activities to build up children's skills and confidence.

It's ideal for extra practice to reinforce their learning in primary school. Enjoy!

CGP

Published by CGP

Editors:
Keith Blackhall, Andy Cashmore, Rachel Craig-McFeely,
Katya Parkes, Jack Tooth

With thanks to Emma Crighton and Juliette Green for the proofreading.

With thanks to Lottie Edwards for the copyright research.

ISBN: 978 1 78908 625 6

Printed by Elanders Ltd, Newcastle upon Tyne.
Cover and graphics used throughout the book © www.edu-clips.com
Cover design concept by emc design ltd.

Text, design, layout and original illustrations © Coordination Group Publications Ltd. (CGP) 2020
All rights reserved.

Contents

ai and oi

The **ai** and **oi** sounds can be written in different ways.

t**ai**l   s**ay**   g**a**m**e**   **oi**l   t**oy**

ai, **ay** and **a_e** can make the **ai** sound.

oi and **oy** can both make the **oi** sound.

CAFE
OPEN

Now Try These

1. Draw lines to join each word to the missing letters.

enj__   s__l   n__sy   l__al

oy   oi

2. Tick the sentences below that use the right spelling of the **ai** sound.

I got a stain on my top. ☐

Bob had to grayt some cheese. ☐

The pot was made out of clay. ☐

2

3. Circle the word in each sentence with the right spelling of the **ai** sound.

The cook wanted to **bake / bayk** a pie.

Anya put **paynt / paint** on the wall.

Dan **paid / pade** for the meal.

I wanted to **stay / stai** on the swing.

4. Can you write these words in the box with the right spelling of the **oi** sound?

r__al

b__l

ann__

sp__l

m__st

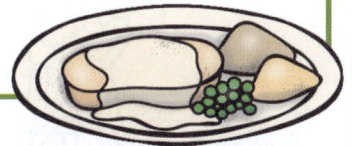

An Extra Challenge

Lisa and Dev have stopped for lunch at a cafe in the park. Can you write down all the things in the picture that contain the **ai** or **oi** sound?

Were these pages a picnic for you? Give a box a tick.

3

The long e sound

The **long e** sound can be written in lots of different ways.

fr**ee**   th**e**m**e**   s**ea**   f**ie**ld

ver**y** ← The **long e** sound written with a **y** always comes at the end of a word.

Now Try These

1. Colour in the pictures where the word is spelt correctly.

clean

sie

carry

whiel

tree

2. Unscramble the letters in bold to make words with the **long e** sound.

The sea is cold and very **depe**. → ....

Jim's parrot is always **uhnrgy**. → ....

I have to fold **teseh** socks. → ....

4

3. Circle the right spelling of each word.

chief / cheef

deleet / delete

emptee / empty

screen / screne

peach / piech

4. Complete each word with the right spelling of the **long e** sound.

Sam put a cherr................ on the cake.

There is a mouse on the deck squ................king.

Nat found seaw................d in her hair.

I couldn't bel................ve Meera's story.

An Extra Challenge

Captain Bigboots has written about a trip she went on with her crew, but she has made some mistakes. How many can you spot? Can you correct them?

I was giving a speach when a bird stole my map. It was in his beke. I told my crew to stop the theef, but they let him get away. I was very angrie. I am going to make them walk the plank to teech them a lesson.

How did you get on? Were these pages plain sailing?

The long i sound

How It Works

The **long i** sound can be written i_e, ie or igh.

i_e

↓

h**i**d**e**

ie

↓

p**ie**

igh

↓

t**igh**t

Now Try These

1. Draw lines to join the words with the same spelling of the **long i** sound.

 tribe

 fried

 right

 mile

 sigh

 lie

2. Circle the word in each sentence with the right spelling of the **long i** sound.

It was a long **driev / drive** to the campsite.

The sun was big and **brite / bright** .

The **spies / spise** were watching Tom.

3. Can you use all the letters on each tent to write a word with the **long i** sound?

_ _ _ _ _

_ _ _ _ _ _

_ _ _ _ _

4. Fill in the gap in each sentence with the right spelling.

Tammy .... her soggy socks.

| dried | dride |

Jess was .... up in the tree.

| hihe | high |

My .... back was late.

| fliet | flight |

It was .... to go home.

| time | tiem |

An Extra Challenge

Fill in the gaps in these words with the **long i** sound.
Then find the words in the wordsearch. Use the pictures to help you.

l __ __ ht

fr __ g __ t

```
L  I  G  H  T  L  O
W  I  K  I  T  E  Q
H  G  P  G  C  Y  U
O  J  E  W  O  A  L
B  I  K  E  I  C  T
N  D  O  U  E  I  I
F  R  I  G  H  T  E
```

k __ t __

t __ __

b __ __ e

Are you delighted with how you did on these pages? Tick a box.

More long vowel sounds

How It Works

The **long o** sound can be written oa, ow, oe or o_e.

b**oa**t   sh**ow**   t**oe**   c**o**d**e**

The **long oo** sound can be written oo, ew, ue or u_e.

f**oo**d   ch**ew**   cl**ue**   r**u**d**e**

Now Try These

1. Can you circle the word with the **long o** sound that's spelt wrong in each sentence?

My cote was soaked after the storm .

I slipped in the snoe and hurt my elbow .

Pavel went hoam because his nose was chilly .

2. Complete each word with the right spelling of the **long oo** sound.

I prefer spring because the weather is c................l.

Rita thr................ a snowball at Dominic.

The film about the ice skater is a tr................ story.

3. Circle the right spelling of each word.

roof / rufe   glew / glue

screw / scrue   flute / floot

spune / spoon   drew / droo

4. Draw lines to join each word to the missing letters, then rewrite the word.

 t__st    oe   ....

 g__s    ow   ....

 bl__    oa   ....

An Extra Challenge

Priya and her friends are talking about a ski race. Can you correct their spelling mistakes to find out what's happening?

I can beat you down this slowp.

Watch out for the goet!

This is my lucky bloo jacket.

Priya will be in a bad mewd if she loses.

Did you keep your cool on these pages? Tick a box.

9

Short vowel sounds

How It Works

Here are some examples of short vowel sounds.

The **short oo** sound can be written u or oo.   put   cook

The **short e** sound can be written e or ea.   egg   bread

Now Try These

1. Colour in the pictures where the word has a **short oo** sound.

wool

float

good

bush

food

truth

2. Unscramble the letters in bold to make words with the **short e** sound.

My face was covered in **swate**.   ➡   ....

We had to **sned** a letter to Mel.   ➡   ....

The doctor took a deep **bretha**.   ➡   ....

3. Circle the word in each sentence with the right spelling of the **short oo** sound.

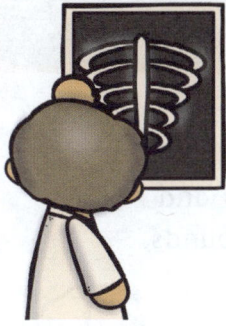

Mandy's **fut / foot** had healed.

Ben had to **push / poosh** the door open.

Doctor Cox had a long **luk / look** at the x-ray.

I got a splinter from a plank of **wud / wood** .

4. Can you write these words in the box with the right spelling of the **short e** sound?

l__g

d__f

m__nt

t__st

f__ther

An Extra Challenge

Use the picture clues to help you spell out the words below.
Can you use each word in a sentence?

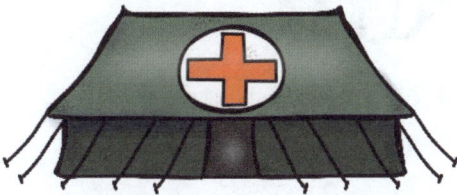

t			t

b			s

h		d

Did these pages treat you well?
Tick a box to show how you did.

11

or, ur and ow

There are lots of different ways to write **or**, **ur** and **ow** sounds.

f**or**t   m**or**e   s**aw**   h**au**l   ←   or, ore, aw and au make **or** sounds.

f**ur**   s**ir**   p**er**son   ←   ur, ir and er make the **ur** sound.

n**ow**   **ou**t   ←   ow and ou make the **ow** sound.

Now Try These

1. Draw lines to join each word to the missing letters.

 l_d

 gr__l

 t_n

 s__th

 ou

 ow

2. Circle the right spelling of each word.

yaun / yawn   hawnt / haunt

snore / snor

crawl / crorl   storm / stawm

cawn / corn

3. Can you use all the letters on each ball to write a word with the **ur** sound?

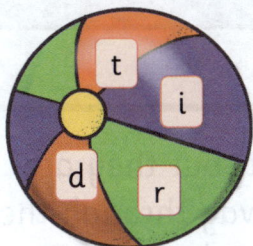 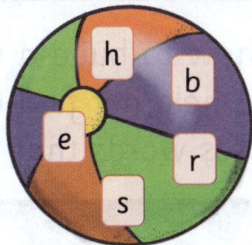  

_ _ _ _ _   _ _ _ _

_ _ _ _ _   _ _ _ _ _

4. Complete each word using the right spelling of the sound in the box.

or sound ➡	Tommy sc................d a point in the game.
ow sound ➡	A lemon tastes very s................r.
ur sound ➡	Ming s................ved dinner to his family.
or sound ➡	Liz put s................ce on her chips.

An Extra Challenge

Using words containing the **or**, **ur** or **ow** sounds, can you write down something that's happening in the picture below? See how many sentences you can make.

Did the or, ur and ow sounds go swimmingly? Tick a box.

Factory fun

Naomi needs to find the instructions for how to build a robot, but they are on the other side of the factory. Can you help her find her way through the building safely? The right path only crosses words that are spelt correctly.

START HERE

groe

rock

shert

tea

funny

slide

lookked

wisper

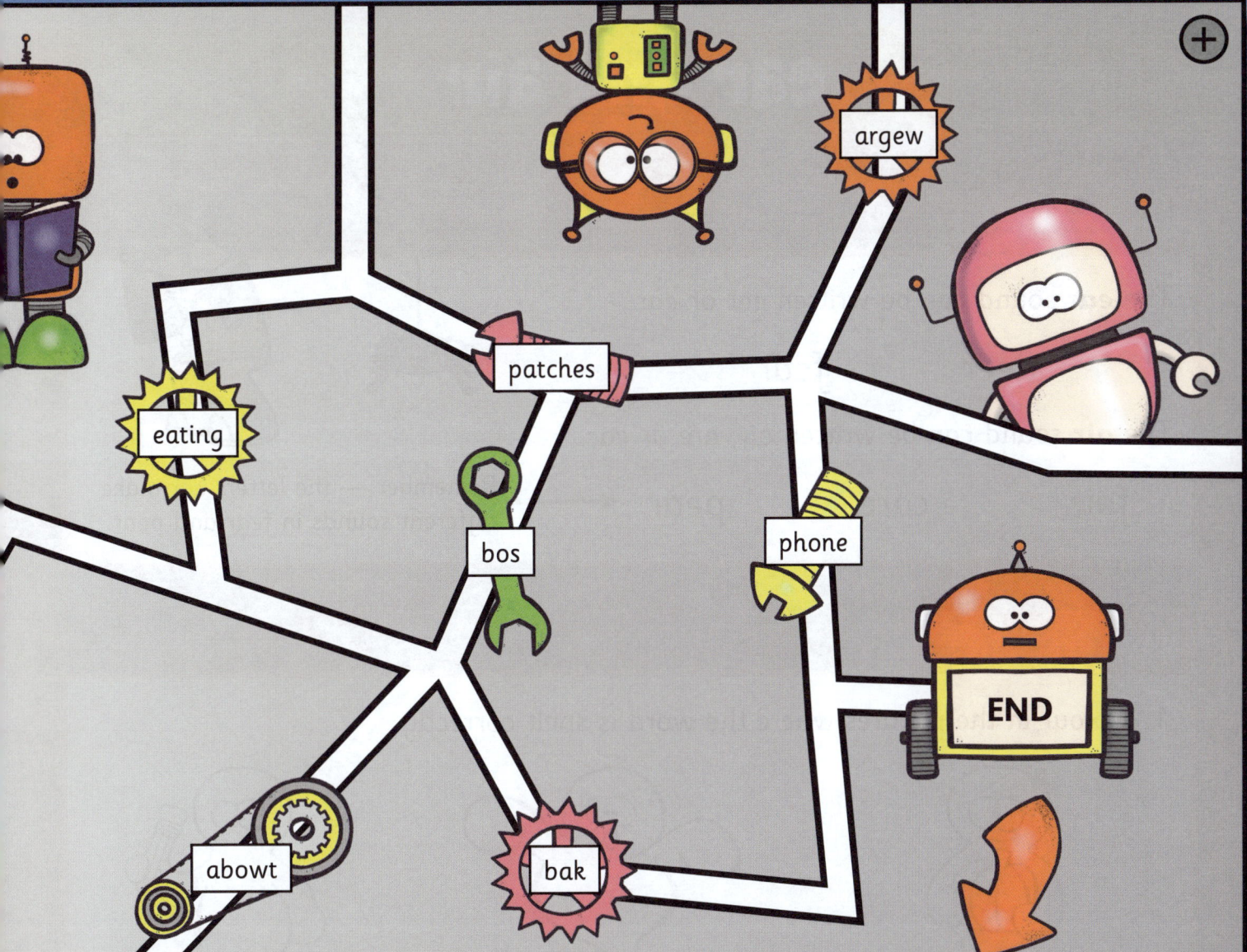

argew

patches

eating

bos

phone

abowt

bak

END

glair

| 1 | 2 | 3 | 4 | 5 | 6 | 7 | 8 |

Oh no! Naomi has the instructions, but she doesn't know which store room the robot parts are in. Can you help her by circling the spelling mistakes below? The number of mistakes gives you the number of the store room.

Dror a plan for your robot. Fech the parts and a tule kit. Dril holes in the metal. Joyn the parts together with some screwes. Now, paynt the robot blue. Your new robot is compleete!

The robot parts are in store room ....

ear and air

How It Works

The **ear** sound can be written eer or ear.

deer   fear

The **air** sound can be written air, are or ear.

fair   care   pear ←

Remember — the letters ear make different sounds in fear and pear.

Now Try These

1. Colour in the pictures where the word is spelt correctly.

gear

spair

chair

repare

swear

cleer

2. Complete each sentence with the right spelling of the **air** sound.

The monster has lots of h........... .

The monster usually w...........s shorts.

It's r.......... to see the monster during the day.

3. Unscramble the letters in the boxes to make words with the **ear** sound. Use the pictures to help you.

| taers | epsar | berad |

....

4. Circle the right spelling of the **ear** or **air** sound to complete each sentence below.

I saw a ghost n........... the school. | ear | eer |

We couldn't h........... what Linda said. | eer | ear |

The b........... likes to sleep in a cave. | ear | air |

An Extra Challenge

Lee and his friends have found a haunted house. Can you correct their spelling mistakes to find out what they are saying?

Were these pages a dream or a nightmare? Put a tick in a box.

Consonant sounds

How It Works

Sometimes the same consonant sounds can be written in different ways.

fish ← f and ph make the **f** sound.

photo ←

well ← w and wh make **w** sounds.

when ←

The **hard c** sound can be written c, k or ck.

cute   **kit**   **back** ← These words all have a **hard c** sound.

Now Try These

1. Draw lines to join each word to the missing letters.

_ow

du__

sna_e

c

k

ck

_itten

_amel

2. Unscramble the letters in bold to make words with the **f** sound.

There are ten sheep at the **mfar**. ➡ ....

A **dphloin** jumped into the air. ➡ ....

The **elapehnt** waved its trunk. ➡ ....

3. Can you complete each word with the right spelling of the **w** sound? Use the pictures to help you.

..........ale ....olf ....isker

4. Circle the right spelling of each word.

wheek / week   cennel / kennel

graph / graf   lick / lic

carrot / karrot   fake / phake   white / wite

An Extra Challenge

Farmer Phil has written a diary entry about his day, but he has made some mistakes. How many can you spot? Can you correct them?

I woke up really early in the morning, put on my soks and shoes and left the house. My pet dog, Rosie, kame running when I wistled. I spent the day loocing after the animals. In the evening, I foned my mum.

How amazing was that animal adventure? Give a box a tick.

Word endings

How It Works

The **f**, **l**, **s** and **z** sounds can be written with double letters at the end of words.

o**ff**   ye**ll**   me**ss**   fi**zz**   ←   These double letters often come after a single vowel in a short word.

The **tch** sound can be written ch or tch.   tor**ch**   ca**tch**

When a word ends with the **v** sound, it is usually written ve.   sa**ve**

Now Try These

1. Colour in the pictures where the word is spelt correctly.

dres

rich

staff

wel

glove

2. Tick the sentence below that uses the right spelling of the **v** sound.
   Rewrite the words that are spelt wrong on the lines without any mistakes.

The prince **gav** away his crown. ☐

They fell in **love** at first sight. ☐

....

....

I **wav** my wand to cast a spell. ☐

20

3. Circle the word in each sentence with the right spelling of the **tch** sound.

The **wich / witch** stirred her potion.

They **teach / teatch** magic at my school.

Zack ate too **mutch / much** cake.

A troll lives in the muddy **ditch / dich** .

The dragons won the football **mach / match** .

4. The words below are spelt wrong.
   Can you rewrite each word with the right spelling?

brav

tal

puf

....

An Extra Challenge

Use the picture clues to help you spell out the words below.
Can you use each word in a sentence?

| d | i | | e |

| c | h | r | | |

| c | | i | | |

Are you a word endings
wizard? Give a box a tick.

21

Adding s and es

A plural is a word for more than one of something.
To make most words into plurals, you add **s** on the end.

one mop ➡ two mop**s**

You add **es** to words that end in **ch**, **sh**, **s**, **ss** or **x** to make them plural.

peach**es**　　　wish**es**　　　bus**es**　　　mess**es**　　　fox**es**

Now Try These

1. Draw lines to join each word to the missing letters.

hat__　　class__　　plant__　　bush__

house__　　box__

s

es

2. Can you turn the words below into plurals by adding **s** or **es**?

stretch ➡ ....

path ➡ ....

flash ➡ ....

3. Complete each word by adding **s** or **es** to the end.

glass.......... book.......... dish.......... toy..........

4. Some verbs end in **s** or **es** too. Circle the words below that are spelt wrong, then rewrite them in the box without any mistakes.

sings

mashs

reades

fixs

misses

chews

cleans

sweepes

An Extra Challenge

Chloe is sorting through some of the things in her room. Can you help her by making a list of all the items below? Make sure that you use the right plurals.

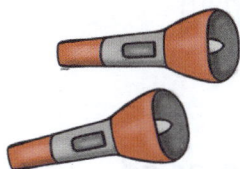   

Are your plurals perfect?
Tick a box to show how you did.

23

Adding ing and ed

Now Try These

1. Can you circle the pictures where the word is spelt correctly?

sprintted

buzzing

postting

pointing

landded

called

2. Unscramble the letters in bold to make a word that ends in **ing** or **ed**.

The crowd **chdeere** loudly. ➡ ....

Jay is **agskin** for the ball. ➡ ....

An army **stemodp** up the hill. ➡ ....

3. Tick the sentences below that use **ing** or **ed** correctly.

It raind all day at the seaside. ☐

I am picking up the bat. ☐

Layla played tennis with Joe. ☐

Harriet is paintting the wall. ☐

4. Rewrite each word below, adding **ing** and **ed** to make new words.

sail → ➕ ing ....
    → ➕ ed ....

borrow → ➕ ing ....
      → ➕ ed ....

An Extra Challenge

Using words that end in **ing** or **ed**, can you describe something from the picture below? How many sentences can you write out?

How did it go? Did you race through these questions?

☐   ☐   ☐

25

Adding er and est

When you add **er** or **est** to most words, the spelling of the original word doesn't change.

 hard

1 + 1

 ✚ er
↓
2 + 2   hard**er**

 ✚ est
↓
3 + 3   hard**est**

Now Try These

1. Can you add **er** to each word to spell these jobs?

build..........   sing..........   clean..........

paint..........   butch..........

2. Rewrite each word below, adding **er** and **est** to make new words.

long ➡ ✚ er ....
      ➡ ✚ est ....

high ➡ ✚ er ....
      ➡ ✚ est ....

3. Can you use the letters in the boxes to make words that end in **er** or **est**? Use the pictures to help you.

`a m s l l t s e`

....

....

`e e a c h t r`

4. Circle the word in bold in each sentence with the right spelling.

Adam was the **fastest / fastst** runner.

The **bankest / banker** counts money.

Ellie is the **shorttest / shortest** girl in the class.

The **gardeneer / gardener** planted a tree.

An Extra Challenge

Arnold, Billy and Yasmin have each thought of a word that ends in **er** or **est**. Can you use their clues to work out the words?

My word starts with c. It means something is the most smart.

My word starts with f. It is a word for someone who cares for animals like cows.

My word starts with f. It means something is the most filled.

Are you the great**est** at adding er and est? Give a box a tick.

😕 ☐　😊 ☐　😉 ☐

Syllables

How It Works

You can break words up into syllables.   Each syllable is like a beat.

spaceship ← This word has 2 syllables.   This word has 3 syllables. → astronaut

space   ship   as   tro   naut

Now Try These

1. Draw lines to show how many syllables each word has.

 star

 1

 banana

 rocket

 2

 alien

 dog

 3

 garden

2. Can you split each of these words up into syllables?

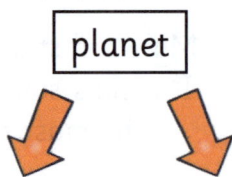 planet

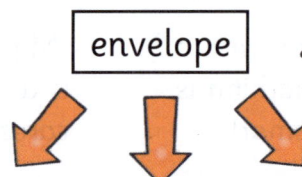 envelope

....

3. Join these syllables together in the right order to make a word.

pen ex sive  ....

pu ter com ➡ ....

cro wave mi ➡ ....

4. Complete each word with the missing syllable. Use the pictures to help you.

 ....et

 ....sers

 butter..........

An Extra Challenge

Marty the Martian has made a list of things with 1, 2 and 3 syllables that he wants to see on Earth. How many more can you come up with for each list?

1 syllable	2 syllables	3 syllables
tree	hamster	motorbike
snake	football	pineapple
beach	pasta	museum

Were these pages out of this world? Put a tick in a box. 🙁 ☐ 🙂 ☐ 😉 ☐

Answers

Pages 2-3 — ai and oi

1. enjoy, soil, noisy, loyal
2. 'I got a stain on my top.' and 'The pot was made out of clay.'
3. You should have circled: bake, paint, paid, stay
4. royal, boil, annoy, spoil, moist

   An Extra Challenge
   Any words that contain the ai or oi sound, e.g. waiter, cake, grape, plate, plane, tray, boy, point, toy, coin.

Pages 4-5 — The long e sound

1. You should have coloured: clean, carry, tree
2. deep, hungry, these
3. You should have circled: chief, delete, empty, screen, peach
4. cherry, squeaking, seaweed, believe

   An Extra Challenge
   The mistakes are: speach (speech), beke (beak), theef (thief), angrie (angry), teech (teach)

Pages 6-7 — The long i sound

1. tribe — mile, fried — lie, right — sigh
2. You should have circled: drive, bright, spies
3. fine, cried, sight
4. You should have written: dried, high, flight, time

   An Extra Challenge
   You should have found: light, fright, kite, tie, bike

Pages 8-9 — More long vowel sounds

1. You should have circled: cote, snoe, hoam
2. cool, threw, true
3. You should have circled: roof, glue, screw, flute, spoon, drew
4. toast, goes, blow

   An Extra Challenge
   The mistakes are: slowp (slope), bloo (blue), goet (goat), mewd (mood)

Pages 10-11 — Short vowel sounds

1. You should have coloured: wool, good, bush
2. sweat, send, breath
3. You should have circled: foot, push, look, wood
4. leg, deaf, meant, test, feather

   An Extra Challenge
   tent, books, head
   Any sentences, e.g. The doctor had lots of books.

Pages 12-13 — or, ur and ow

1. loud, growl, town, south
2. You should have circled: yawn, snore, haunt, crawl, corn, storm
3. dirt, herbs, hurt, swirl
4. scored, sour, served, sauce

   An Extra Challenge
   Any sentences that use words containing the ow sound, the or sound or the ur sound, e.g. The turtle is wearing a crown.

Pages 14-15 — Factory fun

The path should go through these words: funny, slide, tea, rock, eating, patches, phone
You should have circled: dror (draw), fech (fetch), tule (tool), dril (drill), joyn (join), screwes (screws), paynt (paint), compleete (complete). The robot parts are in store room 8.

Pages 16-17 — ear and air

1. You should have coloured: gear, chair, swear

2. hair, wears, rare
3. tears, spear, beard
4. near, hear, bear

   An Extra Challenge
   The mistakes are: dair (dare), scaired (scared), yeers (years), bewear (beware)

Pages 18-19 — Consonant sounds

1. cow, duck, snake, kitten, camel
2. farm, dolphin, elephant
3. whale, wolf, whisker
4. You should have circled: week, kennel, graph, lick, carrot, fake, white

   An Extra Challenge
   The mistakes are: soks (socks), kame (came), wistled (whistled), loocing (looking), foned (phoned)

Pages 20-21 — Word endings

1. You should have coloured: rich, staff, glove
2. You should have ticked: They fell in love at first sight.
   You should have written: gave, wave
3. You should have circled: witch, teach, much, ditch, match
4. brave, tall, puff

   An Extra Challenge
   drive, church, cliff
   Any sentences, e.g. I drive the red car along the road.

Pages 22-23 — Adding s and es

1. hats, classes, plants, bushes, houses, boxes
2. stretches, paths, flashes
3. glasses, books, dishes, toys
4. You should have circled and corrected: mashs (mashes), reades (reads), fixs (fixes), sweepes (sweeps)

   An Extra Challenge
   e.g. Two torches, a pair of shoes, two brushes, a bunch of flowers, two dolls, three mugs and two dresses.

Pages 24-25 — Adding ing and ed

1. You should have circled: buzzing, pointing, called
2. cheered, asking, stomped
3. 'I am picking up the bat.' and 'Layla played tennis with Joe.'
4. sailing, sailed, borrowing, borrowed

   An Extra Challenge
   Any sentences that use words that end in ing or ed, e.g. Mum pushed the pram in the park.

Pages 26-27 — Adding er and est

1. builder, painter, singer, butcher, cleaner
2. longer, longest, higher, highest
3. smallest, teacher
4. You should have circled: fastest, banker, shortest, gardener

   An Extra Challenge
   cleverest, farmer, fullest

Pages 28-29 — Syllables

1. star/dog — 1, rocket/garden — 2, banana/alien — 3
2. planet — pla net/plan et, envelope — en ve lope/en vel ope
3. expensive, computer, microwave
4. jacket, trousers, butterfly

   An Extra Challenge
   Any words that contain 1, 2 or 3 syllables.

EPFS1Q11